COOL CAREERS WITHOUT COLLEGE
FOR PEOPLE WHO LOVE
ANIMALS

NEW

COOL CAREERS WITHOUT COLLEGE
FOR PEOPLE WHO LOVE
ANIMALS

CAROL HAND

ROSEN
PUBLISHING®

New York

Published in 2014 by The Rosen Publishing Group, Inc.
29 East 21st Street, New York, NY 10010

First Edition

Library of Congress Cataloging-in-Publication Data

Hand, Carol, 1945- author.
Cool careers without college for people who love animals/Carol Hand.—First edition.
    pages cm.—(New cool careers without college)
Includes bibliographical references and index.
ISBN 978-1-4777-1822-3 (library binding)
1. Animal specialists—Vocational guidance—United States—Juvenile literature.
I. Title.
SF80.H36 2014
636.023'73—dc23

2013012104

Manufactured in the United States of America

CPSIA Compliance Information: Batch #W14YA: For further information, contact Rosen Publishing, New York, New York, at 1-800-237-9932.
A portion of the material in this book has been derived from *Cool Careers Without College for Animal Lovers* by Chris Hayhurst.

CONTENTS

INTRODUCTION

Do you spend hours playing with your dog or cat? Do you make friends with your neighbors' pets or take in stray animals? Do you save baby birds that fall from their nests? Do you watch wildlife programs and dream of going on safari? If any—or all—of these things apply to you, you might want to consider a job where you can work with animals all the time.

For any animal career, you'll need great love and compassion for animals. Sometimes, this is all you need. Sometimes, you might take courses to become certified in a special field. You must also gain experience working with animals. Animals can't speak in words, but they have their own languages. It takes patience, empathy, and great observational skills to figure out what animals need and what they are trying to say.

If you have pets, you are already getting experience. But the best way is to volunteer.

The first requirement for a career working with animals is to love them, and a great way to learn about animals is to take care of your own pets.

Every animal agency, from the humane society to the zoo to your local vet, needs caring, reliable volunteers. The work is not glamorous. Often, you will be cleaning cages or dog runs or mucking out barns or stables. But as you work around animals, you'll come to understand them. Also, read all you can about the kinds of animals you want to work with.

As you gain experience, you might be offered a paying job, internship, or apprenticeship. This might turn into a career. You'll probably never get rich working with animals, but the rewards are great. How would it make you feel to rescue abused pets, work with wild animals, train Seeing Eye dogs, ride horses, or keep bees? If any of these possibilities make you think, "Yes, I'd love to do that!" then keep reading.

CHAPTER 1

WORKING WITH A VET

If you have a pet, chances are you've seen your local veterinarian at work, examining pets, doing tests, and prescribing medicine. Perhaps you've thought it would be fun to work as a vet. But you don't have to be a vet to work in a veterinary hospital. You probably noticed that your vet has one or more assistants.

RECEPTIONIST AND VETERINARY ASSISTANT

As a receptionist in a vet's office, you greet pets and owners, pull charts, and take information. You answer phones, make appointments, and talk to owners about their pet's condition. Interaction with animals mostly occurs in the front office.

In smaller vet clinics, the receptionist may double as a veterinary assistant. In larger offices, these two positions are separate. As a veterinary assistant, you help the vet by moving pets from the waiting room to the examination room, weighing them, or holding and calming them during procedures. You may prepare food, care for animals kept overnight, and

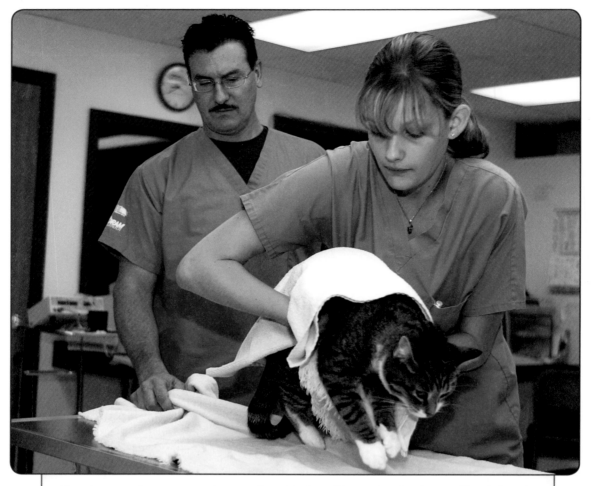

Veterinary assistants must be comfortable handling animals who are ill or injured. Here, a vet assistant soothes a cat who has just had a medical procedure.

take dogs for walks. Veterinary assistants are non-licensed. Some are trained on the job. Others take training programs at community or vocational colleges. Training lasts less than a year and certifies you as a veterinary assistant.

VETERINARY TECHNICIAN

Veterinary technicians, or vet techs, are supervised by a veterinarian and are similar to nurses. You might take temperatures and give injections. You might clean teeth, develop X-rays, or draw blood samples. You might even splint a broken leg or wrap a wound. You prepare for, assist in, and clean up after surgeries. You monitor animals after surgery, change dressings, and report problems to the veterinarian.

Vet techs must complete a two-year associate's degree program offered by community colleges and accredited by the American Veterinary Medical Association (AVMA). These programs include courses in animal science, teach practical

IT'S NOT 9 TO 5!

If you're considering an animal career, remember that animals don't operate on human schedules. Very few animal jobs are Monday through Friday, 9:00 to 5:00. Pets get sick or hit by cars on weekends. A horse delivers her foal at 3:00 AM. Dogs have to be walked several times a day—every day. Some animals need to be fed several times a day. If animals are in trouble, they need to be rescued right away—not Monday morning when it's more convenient. So if you really want a career working with animals, be prepared to work long hours, including weekends, night shifts, and occasional all-nighters.

skills, and provide hands-on experience with animals.

KENNEL WORKER

Many pet owners board their pets at a kennel when they go away, and kennels are often associated with veterinary clinics. Kennel workers provide basic pet care. You'll receive pets from their owners and transfer them to their kennels. You will clean cages and dog runs, fill food and water bowls, and exercise and play with the animals. Pets left at kennels can be very nervous. They are in an unfamiliar environment surrounded by strange animals, and their owners have disappeared. Your job is to make them as comfortable as possible.

EDUCATION REQUIRED

You can start preparing for a career working with a veterinarian while

Happy dogs play in the water at a boarding kennel and day care center in Carson City, Nevada. These establishments care for pets when their owners must work or go out of town.

you're still in middle or high school. Courses in science, math, computers, biology, and animal science will help. Volunteer at a local vet hospital, kennel, or animal shelter. You can work as a secretary or a kennel worker with a high school diploma and can receive on-the-job training to be a vet assistant. After completing a vet tech program, you must pass the state veterinary technician exam. Depending on the state, this makes you a registered, licensed, or certified veterinary technician. You will need this credential to be hired by larger vet clinics, especially in large cities.

JOB PROSPECTS

The U.S. Bureau of Labor Statistics reports that the need for veterinary assistants and caretakers such as kennel workers will grow rapidly during the next ten years. The need for licensed vet techs will grow even faster, especially in rural areas. Vet techs work at private veterinary hospitals, zoos, universities, humane societies, or animal control operations.

WHAT IT'S LIKE

Angie and Jennifer work at an animal hospital in Pittsburg, Kansas. Angie's title is secretary, but that doesn't begin to describe her duties. "I've done pretty much everything except grooming—and being a vet," she says. The clinic doesn't

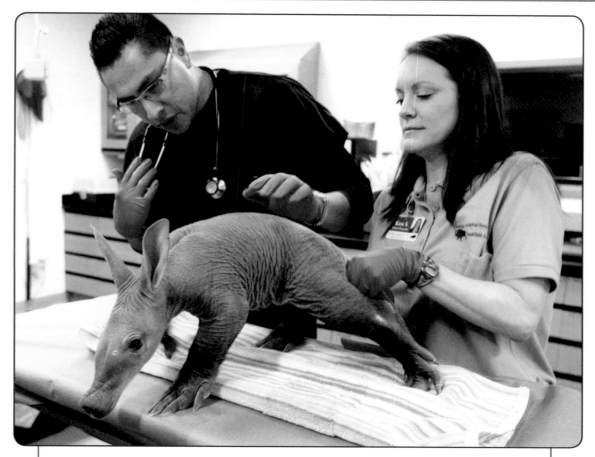

Associate veterinarian Carlos Sanchez and vet technician Kate Sladek examine a five-week-old baby aardvark born on January 12, 2011, at the Chicago Zoological Society's Brookfield Zoo in Brookfield, Illinois.

hire separate vet assistants, so Angie has learned many other skills. She gives injections and assists during surgery. But, she points out, her duties also include mopping floors and taking out the trash. Also, she and other clinic workers take turns caring for "overnight" animals. Each is on duty about one weekend a month.

Jennifer is the "clinic floater." She works wherever she is needed. She is responsible for the clinic's boarding kennel. She takes the dogs out three times a day, cleans cages and floors, and feeds and bathes animals. She also works in the vet clinic, making up "surgery packs" of instruments and supplies. She helps with exams and surgeries and works at the front desk.

Both Angie and Jennifer are constantly learning. Jennifer is taking an online course in animal dentistry. The clinic's two veterinarians have taught them to draw blood and identify parasites under the microscope. They both love their jobs. Jennifer especially loves working in the kennel. Angie enjoys working with both the animals and their owners. She says, "This is the best job I've ever had. It's very satisfying to make people happy by keeping their pets healthy."

FOR MORE INFORMATION

BOOKS

Anderson, Laurie Halse. *Acting Out* #14 (Vet Volunteers).
   New York, NY: Puffin Books (Penguin Books LTD), 2012.
This is one of a fiction series on kids who work to save pets.

Jackson, Donna M. *ER Vets: Life in an Animal Emergency
   Room*. San Anselmo, CA: Sandpiper Press LLC, 2009.
This illustrated book describes what happens behind
   the scenes when injured animals go to the vet.

Rose, Rebecca, and Carin A. Smith. *Career Choices for
   Veterinary Technicians: Opportunities for Animal Lovers*.
   Lakewood, CO: AAHA Press, 2009.
This book gives details on the many career paths for
   vet techs.

MAGAZINES

AJVR, American Journal of Veterinary Research
1931 N. Meacham Road, Suite 100
Schaumburg, IL 60173-4360
(847) 925-8070, ext 6752
Web site: avmajournals.avma.org/loi/ajvr

This is a scientific research journal for veterinary medicine; available online.

JAVMA, Journal of the Veterinary Medical Association
1931 N. Meacham Road, Suite 100
Schaumburg, IL 60173-4360
(847) 925-8070 or (800) 248-2862
Web site: avmajournals.avma.org/loi/javma
This is a scientific journal for veterinary medicine; available online.

Veterinary Technician Magazine
https://www.vetlearn.com
This magazine has articles geared to vet techs.

ORGANIZATIONS

American Animal Hospital Association (AAHA)
12575 W. Bayaud Avenue
Lakewood, CO 80228
(303) 986-2800
Web site: https://www.aahanet.org

American Veterinary Medical Association
1931 North Meacham Road, Suite 100
Schaumburg, IL 60173-4360

(800) 248-2862
Web site: https://www.avma.org/Pages/home.aspx

Canadian Veterinary Medical Association
339 Booth Street
Ottawa, ON K1R 7K1
Canada
(613) 236-1162
Web site: http://www.canadianveterinarians.net

North American Veterinary Technician
Association (NAVTA)
P.O. Box 1227
Albert Lea, MN 56007
(888) 99-NAVTA (62882)
Web site: http://www.navta.net

WEB SITES
Due to the changing nature of Internet links, Rosen
Publishing has developed an online list of Web sites
related to the subject of this book. This site is updated
regularly. Please use this link to access the list:

http://www.rosenlinks.com/CCWC/Anim

CHAPTER 2

WORKING IN AN ANIMAL SHELTER

Stray, abused, and neglected dogs and cats often end up in animal shelters, also called humane shelters or humane societies. Animal shelter employees protect animals and work for animal welfare. They run shelters, feed and care for the animals, and find new homes for them. It's not easy—animals are often sick and some die. Some must be put to sleep. Still, shelter workers find it very rewarding to nurse an animal back to health and see it off to a new, loving home.

Most animal shelters are nonprofit organizations. They make no extra money but just cover expenses—enough to pay employees' salaries and keep things running. So if you decide to work in a shelter, don't expect a fat paycheck. You should be there because you love helping animals, not for the money.

SHELTER EMPLOYEES

Entry-level shelter employees are animal caretakers. They feed animals, provide water, and clean cages. They keep records of when animals are checked in and when they are released to new homes. They record all tests, medications, and treatments. They also work with the public. They answer questions about humane pet care and show animals available for adoption.

Most shelter animals are domesticated cats and dogs. But some shelters care for farm animals, and others specialize in wild animals. The latter are usually called wildlife refuges or wildlife rehabilitation centers.

Other shelter workers include humane investigators, humane educators, and shelter managers. Humane investigators

A volunteer from California helps care for some of the eight hundred pets taken in by the Joplin (Missouri) Animal Adoption and Rescue Center after a devastating tornado in May 2011.

do detective work. They try to find out how animals have ended up abandoned or injured. Humane educators teach the public about humane treatment of animals. They travel around the community and teach people how to be responsible pet owners. The shelter manager supervises employees and makes sure the shelter runs smoothly. She must also decide when to euthanize an animal. This is done by a vet, who gives the animal a special drug that painlessly puts it to death. Euthanasia is done only as a last resort, but it is stressful for the employees.

EDUCATION REQUIRED

Animal caretakers and shelter workers require no special training, but helpful courses are offered through the Humane Society of the United States (HSUS), the American Humane Association (AHA), and the National Animal Control Association (NACA). These courses cover topics like how to deal with abusive pet owners, how and when to euthanize an animal, and how to work with wild animals. The HSUS offers workshops in humane education and an online certified humane education specialist

A volunteer feeds tigers at the Wild Animal Sanctuary in Keenesburg, Colorado. The sanctuary is home to 290 large carnivores that were confiscated from illegal and abusive situations.

program. AHA offers downloadable programs for humane education.

Practical experience will help you land an entry-level animal shelter job. You can get experience by volunteering at a shelter or taking a summer position, paid or unpaid. But the best training for animal shelter employees is on the job. As you gain experience you'll be able to move into management positions. Eventually, you might find yourself running the shelter.

JOB PROSPECTS

Many people get pets and don't know how to care for them. Unfortunately, these pets often end up neglected, abused, or on the street. Without animal shelters, they'd have nowhere to go. For this reason, the Bureau of Labor Statistics expects demand for animal care workers to grow rapidly in the near future. Job stress leads to high turnover rates, which also increases the demand.

WHAT IT'S LIKE

Melissa is the director of the SEK Humane Society in Pittsburg, Kansas. The shelter is almost totally dependent on donations. "We're constantly doing fund-raisers," Melissa says. "We have to work hard to keep things going."

Their cats and dogs arrive from all over. Some are strays; others are left behind when people move or die. The sheriff brings in animals from the county, and city animal control workers bring those picked up in town. Melissa is relieved about this—the city used to keep stray animals ten days and then euthanize them. But a recently hired officer set up a co-operative program, and now the animals are brought to SEK.

There are also drop-offs. "A lot of really bad people just drop off animals in the middle of the night," Melissa says. "I get a call and have to come and catch them and bring them into the shelter." Recently, she rescued a pair of boxers, Andy and Amelia. Amelia was trusting and came to her right away, but Melissa spent forty-five minutes sitting quietly in the dark, coaxing Andy until he finally came close enough to be leashed. Like all the shelter's animals, they will stay until they find homes. Usually the shelter has about a hundred cats and dogs. Most are adopted fairly quickly, but one small Chihua-hua mix has lived at the shelter for two years.

They only euthanize animals when absolutely necessary, such as medical situations when nothing can be done. "Making the decision to euthanize is the hardest thing I have to do," Melissa says, "but sometimes there's no choice."

Melissa works hard, and her job is demanding. But there is a big upside. "Rescuing a dog from a bad situation and finding them a perfect 'forever home' is the greatest feeling in the world," she says.

FOR MORE INFORMATION

BOOKS

Boneham, Sheila Webster. *Rescue Matters: How to Find, Foster, and Rehome Companion Animals: A Guide for Volunteers and Organizers*. Crawford, CO: Alpine Publications, Inc., 2009.
Complete guide to starting and running a rescue shelter.

Daffron, Susan C. *Publicity to the Rescue: How to Get More Attention for Your Animal Shelter, Humane Society, or Rescue Group to Raise Awareness, Increase Donations, Recruit Volunteers, and Boost Adoptions*. Sandpoint, ID: Logical Expressions, Inc., 2011.
Tips on how to get publicity and the benefits (other than money) it brings to a shelter.

Kloth, Michael. *Shelter Cats*. London, England: Merrell Publishers, 2010.
Photo album featuring cats and kittens left at shelters.

Kloth, Michael. *Shelter Puppies*. London, England: Merrell Publishers, 2011.
Photo album featuring unique puppies left at shelters.

Ross, Mark. *Animal Shelter Portraits*. Brooklyn, NY: Mark Batty Publisher, 2012.

This book features stories of animals stranded at kill shelters because no homes can be found for them.

MAGAZINES

Animal Sheltering Magazine
The Humane Society of the United States
2100 L Street NW
Washington, DC 20037
(202) 452-1100
Web site: http://www.humanesociety.org
Bimonthly color magazine with articles about shelters and animal protection.

Animal Tracks Magazine
Animal Humane Society
Web site: http://www.animalhumanesociety.org/
aboutus/animaltracks
Magazine of the Animal Humane Society, published three times per year.

ORGANIZATIONS

The American Humane Association
1400 16th Street NW, Suite 360
Washington, DC 20036

(800) 227-4645
Web site: http://www.americanhumane.org

The American Society for the Prevention of Cruelty
    to Animals
424 East 92nd Street
New York, NY 10128-6804
(212) 876-7700
Web site: http://www.aspca.org

The Humane Society of the United States
2100 L Street NW
Washington, DC 20037
(202) 452-1100
Web site: http://www.humanesociety.org

National Animal Control Association
101 N. Church Street
Olathe, KS 66061
(913) 768-1319
Web site: http://www.nacanet.org

People for the Ethical Treatment of Animals (PETA)
501 Front Street
Norfolk, VA 23510

(757) 622-PETA (7382)
Web site: http://www.peta.org

The World Society for the Protection of Animals (WSPA)
   WSPA USA
Nelson Tower Building
450 Seventh Avenue, 31st Floor
New York, NY 10123
(800) 883-WSPA (9772)
Web site: http://www.wspa-international.org

WEB SITES

Due to the changing nature of Internet links, Rosen Publishing has developed an online list of Web sites related to the subject of this book. This site is updated regularly. Please use this link to access the list:

http://www.rosenlinks.com/CCWC/Anim

CHAPTER 3

WORKING IN ANIMAL RESCUE

Neglected or abused animals often end up at shelters or humane societies—but how do they get there? That's the job of animal rescue personnel. If mistreatment of animals horrifies you and you want to do something about it, a career in animal rescue might be for you. But, besides having compassion for animals, you must be able to work with people—sometimes difficult, angry people—without losing your cool. You must be able to control your emotions because you will see animals in cruel situations and will need to do whatever is necessary to make them safe.

Animal cruelty investigators work for shelters or humane societies. Animal control officers, or "animal cops," work for the police department.

ANIMAL CRUELTY INVESTIGATOR

Animal cruelty investigators check into situations where people might be mistreating animals or animals might be living in inhumane conditions. Often people call an animal shelter if they think this is happening. The shelter sends out an investigator, who interviews both the person who made the complaint and the person keeping the animals. The investigator also views the animals and their living conditions. If he determines that neglect or abuse is occurring, it is his job to take care of the animals. He gives them food and water and informs the animals' owner of the humane laws being broken. Sometimes, he removes the animals from the situation and takes them back to the shelter. Sometimes, investigators look into animal exploitation, such as dog and cock fights. They may cooperate with local police or refer the matter to the police for resolution.

For each situation, the animal cruelty investigator takes photos and writes a report. This documentation may be used to prosecute people for animal neglect or abuse.

ANIMAL COP (ANIMAL CONTROL OFFICER)

Animal control officers pick up lost or stray animals or those causing problems for people. The country's most advanced "animal cop" program is probably the Humane Law Enforcement (HLE) Division of the New York State ASPCA (American Society for the Prevention of Cruelty to Animals). New York's HLE officers must be eligible for

Animal control officers help a veterinary technician feed a starving horse, one of twenty-eight removed from an abusive owner. When rescued, the horses were standing in manure up to their knees.

certification as New York State peace officers (similar to police officers but with different firearm licenses and other requirements). HLE accepts officers certified by the National Animal Control Association (NACA). They prefer prior experience as police officers, peace officers, or park rangers.

HLE officers have the same powers as police officers—they investigate, collect evidence, arrest people, and carry guns, clubs, and pepper spray. Animal cops always work with partners. They rescue all kinds of animals, domestic and wild, large and small.

EDUCATION REQUIRED

Animal rescue jobs require specific skills and abilities. Besides love and compassion for animals, you must be strongly committed to animal welfare. You must be

DEALING WITH EMOTIONS

People in animal-related jobs care deeply about animals. This often leads to emotional stress. One very stressful situation is the need to euthanize a pet or an abused animal. Most employees become very attached to the animals and feel grief if they must be euthanized. In animal cruelty situations, anger is also part of the job. You will see animals being cruelly mistreated and often meet the people responsible. You must learn to control your emotions during the job. Outside the job, find ways to let go of your stress. Also, seek support from friends, support groups, or professionals.

able to make difficult decisions, such as deciding whether to remove an animal from its owner. You must have excellent communication and people skills, including the ability to talk calmly with difficult people and mediate disputes.

College courses or two-year degrees in psychology, sociology, animal science, or criminal justice are helpful. Some schools, humane societies, and shelters offer courses in animal cruelty investigation. NACA offers a series of courses at regional locations to prepare animal control officers. These courses can be taken by anyone eighteen years of age or older. Successful completion of the first two courses leads to national certification.

JOB PROSPECTS

The outlook for future animal rescue personnel is good. There are more and more animals in need of rescue and compassionate people are needed to help. If you start working at an animal shelter and gain experience with animals, you can work up to assisting in animal rescue, even without further education. But the more training you get, the better prepared you will be to participate in this vital career.

Jobs vary by state and city. The best way to start in animal rescue is to contact your local humane society, animal control office, or police department. They can tell you what opportunities

Animal control officer Marissa Bostick captures a stray pit bull found roaming in a Houston, Texas, neighborhood. Pit bulls have a reputation for attacking people and are often used in illegal dog fighting.

are available and what training and certification you will require.

Salaries will be low, especially in an animal shelter or humane society. Animal control officers will make the same amount as other police officers at the same level.

WHAT IT'S LIKE

Tim Rickey has been the ASPCA's senior director of field investigations and response since 2010. He worked for the Missouri Animal Cruelty Task Force before joining the ASPCA. Rickey says, "I have always been very passionate about animals, and I started working at a humane society when I was sixteen. I went on to an eleven-year-career in animal control, where I became very involved in cruelty investigations."

In 2009, Rickey worked with the FBI, USDA, and Missouri Highway Patrol to rescue 500 dogs during a dog-fighting investigation. Thousands more dogs were saved from participating in what Rickey describes as a "barbaric form of animal cruelty." "The best part of this job," he says, "is knowing that every day we are able to help animals. It is very rewarding to know that when my team arrives to a property where animals have been abused, the animals will be safe."

FOR MORE INFORMATION

BOOKS

Rogers, Tom. *A Working Guide to Animal Control and Enforcement*. Frederick, MD: PublishAmerica, 2009.
This book tells the story of how one community solved the problem of animal control and rising expenses.

Zindler, Shirley. *The Secret Life of Dog Catchers: An Animal Control Officer's Passion to Make a Difference.* CreateSpace Independent Publishing Platform, 2012.
This is the true story of an animal control officer, with daring rescues and funny situations.

MAGAZINES

Animal Sheltering (for shelter and rescue professionals)
The Humane Society of the United States (HSUS)
2100 L Street NW
Washington, DC 20037
(202) 452-110
Web site: http://www.humanesociety.org
Bimonthly color magazine with articles about shelters and animal protection.

Modern Dog
Modern Dog Inc.
Suite 202 - 343 Railway St.
Vancouver, BC V6A 1A4
Canada
(604) 734-3131 or (866) 734-3131
Web site: http://www.moderndogmagazine.com/
   articles/give-me-shelter/564
Articles on dogs, including sheltering and rescue, breed
   profiles, and photos.

Pet Folio Magazine
P.O. Box 8997
Reno, NV 89507
(775) 560-4242
Web site: http://www.petfoliomagazine.com/index.html
Nevada-based online publication on animal rescue, cov-
   ering horses, cats, and dogs.

ORGANIZATIONS
American Society for the Prevention of Cruelty to
   Animals (ASPCA)
424 E. 92nd Street
New York, NY 10128-6804
(212) 876-7700
Web site: http://www.aspca.org

National Animal Control Association (NACA)
101 N. Church Street
Olathe, KS 66061
(913) 768-1319
Web site: http://www.nacanet.org/index.html

National Animal Rescue and Sheltering Coalition
(336) 496-2772
Web site: http://narsc.net

National Association of Pet Rescue Professionals (NAPRP)
c/o Logical Expressions, Inc.
311 Fox Glen Road
Sandpoint, ID 83864
(520) 333-5341
Web site: http://www.naprp.com/About/tabid/57/
   Default.aspx

WEB SITES

Due to the changing nature of Internet links, Rosen
Publishing has developed an online list of Web sites
related to the subject of this book. This site is updated
regularly. Please use this link to access the list:

http://www.rosenlinks.com/CCWC/Anim

CHAPTER 4

TRAINING SERVICE OR ASSISTANCE DOGS

Service or assistance dogs act as helpers or guides for disabled people. But they're not born with the ability to obey their owners and do cool tricks. They must be taught hundreds of commands. Professional assistance dog trainers work closely with both humans and dogs. They not only train the dogs, they also teach their eventual owners how to interact with their assistance dogs. The job requires a tremendous amount of patience and responsibility.

WHAT ASSISTANCE DOGS DO

People with many different kinds of disabilities use assistance or service dogs. Blind people use Seeing Eye dogs, who guide them along sidewalks, streets, and hallways while avoiding obstacles like people, cars, walls, and open doors. "Hearing dogs" assist deaf and hearing-impaired people. The dogs are trained to understand sign language and to react to sounds, including doorbells, telephones, fire alarms, and babies' cries. Mobility assistance dogs help people in wheelchairs or those who have difficulty walking. They open and close doors, turn lights off and on, and pick up and carry items ranging from keys to groceries.

Service dogs, also called medical response dogs, respond to specific medical situations, such as seizures or psychiatric conditions. They recognize warning signs or behaviors before something happens and warn the person or a caretaker.

HOW ASSISTANCE DOGS ARE TRAINED

The breed of dog used depends on the type of service. See-ing Eye dogs and mobility assistance dogs are often golden or Labrador retrievers or German shepherds. These dogs are people-oriented, helpful rather than protective, not overly active, and easy to groom. In other words, they're easy for a physically disabled person to manage. Most hearing dogs are rescued from shelters. They are usually small to medium sized. They must be energetic and able to respond instantly to sounds. Typical hearing dogs are mixes of terriers, poodles, cockers, Lhasa apsos, shih tzus, and Chihuahuas.

Training a service dog is an intense process. At Leader Dogs for the Blind, an instructor trains dog and student (apprentice instructor) together for approximately four months. During the first month, you teach the dog to walk with a harness. During month two, you teach it to detect

curbs, avoid obstacles, and navigate traffic. During month three, you go into the city and learn more complicated techniques such as using escalators and traveling on trains. Finally, you, your instructor, and the dog work to train the client who will receive the dog.

Training procedures are similar for all types of service dogs. Trainers use positive reinforcement techniques, which reward the dog for correct behaviors. The skills taught differ for each type of service. According to Assistance Dogs International (ADI), training the dog is the easy part. Training a client with physical or mental disabilities can be difficult. The client must learn what the dog can do, what signals it understands, and how to handle it.

You have to love both dogs and people to be an assistance dog trainer. In many cases you'll be around the dogs—anywhere from one to a dozen—full-time. You must have great patience, common sense, and enthusiasm. You must be willing to work hard and get dirty. You'll not only grow close to your canine friends, but you'll also meet and work with amazing people.

EDUCATION REQUIRED

According to ADI, a well-trained dog requires one to two hours of training per day over six months—that is, 180 to 360 hours total. The trainer requires a three-year apprenticeship.

White, a mobility assistance dog shown here with his trainer, Amanda Heidenreiter, is being trained to bring items such as water bottles to people in wheelchairs.

THERAPY ANIMAL TEAMS

One way to decide if you would make a good service dog trainer is to volunteer with your pet. Pet Partners offers training on animal handling and helps you and your pet become a registered therapy animal team. As you visit hospitals, nursing homes, and classrooms, you will get a firsthand look at how pets can improve people's lives just by being themselves. Pet therapy animals are not just dogs; they can include cats, guinea pigs, miniature horses, and even llamas. Of course, if your pet is a horse or a llama, patients will have to come to you—and for some patients, this can be arranged.

Individual organizations certify their trainers and dogs. Members of ADI certify apprentices using the ADI Public Access Test. But for now, formal education or certification is not required to become an assistance dog trainer.

The best way to learn how to train assistance dogs is through hands-on experience. If there's a dog-training business in your area—even if it's just a regular pet-dog-training facility—see if you can volunteer or work as an apprentice to a practicing professional trainer. Another good way to see if this is something you really want to do is volunteering to work with disabled people. As you come to understand their needs, you'll see why assistance dogs are so important to their lives.

JOB PROSPECTS

People are beginning to realize how important dogs can be in the lives of disabled people. Assistance dogs are now allowed on airplanes, in restaurants, in stores—anywhere their owners go. With the growing acceptance of and increased demand for assistance dogs, the job market for professional trainers looks great. But salaries in this field are very low. Most training companies are nonprofits. They have little money and must struggle to raise the funds required to buy and train the dogs. Employees are there for the love of their work and the desire to help people, not to get rich.

WHAT IT'S LIKE

Karen, an assistance dog trainer for Assistance Dogs of the West in Santa Fe, New Mexico, says:

> The dogs are always learning. That's why they live with me. If I leave the bathroom door open, they push it shut for me. If I drop the keys at the front door, they pick them up. If I'm feeding other dogs, they have to wait. If I'm eating dinner, they need to be under the table and not begging. If I'm cooking, they can't be sitting right under the stove.

Leah, a certified hearing dog, accompanies her owner to a race at the Daytona International Speedway. Hearing dogs are often small dogs such as Chihuahuas.

The dogs are a wonderful part of the business. It's incredible to work with them and teach them, but I think what it's really about are the clients—the people with disabilities. Teaching the disabled to work with the dogs is more important than training the dogs. And to watch the dogs go work with somebody who really needs them is touching to me.

FOR MORE INFORMATION

BOOKS

Davis, Marcie, and Melissa Bunnell. *Working Like Dogs: The Service Dog Guidebook*. Loveland, CO: Alpine Publications, 2007.
Personal stories, practical tips, and other resources about service dogs.

Long, Lorie. *A Dog Who's Always Welcome: Assistance and Therapy Dog Trainers Teach You How to Socialize and Train Your Companion Dog*. Hoboken, NJ: Howell Book House (John Wiley & Sons), 2008.
Describes service dog training and shows how everyone can use the same techniques to train their dogs.

Nordensson, Stewart, and Lydia Kelley. *Teamwork, Book I: A Training Manual for People with Disabilities*. Revised and Expanded Edition. Tucson, AZ: Top Dog Publications, 2007.
Dog-training manual written for people with disabilities to train their own dog; covers basic obedience and canine behavior.

Nordensson, Stewart, and Lydia Kelley. *Teamwork II: Dog Training Manual for People with Disabilities* (Service

Exercises). Revised and Expanded Edition. Tucson, AZ: Top Dog Publications, 2010.
Sequel to book I, covering specific service exercises such as retrieving objects.

Vanfleet, Risë. *The Human Half of Dog Training: Collaborating with Clients to Get Results*. Wenatchee, WA: Direct Book Service, 2012.
Describes how to work with clients who will receive trained service dogs.

MAGAZINES

APDT Chronicle of the Dog
Association of Pet Dog Trainers
104 South Calhoun Street
Greenville, SC 29601
Web site: http://www.apdt.com/contact
Bimonthly magazine with latest training techniques and other helpful information.

Interactions – Archives
Pet Partners (formerly Delta Society)
289 Perimeter Road East
Renton, WA 98055-1329

Web site: http://www.petpartners.org/interactions
Archives of recent issues, with articles on therapy animals.

ORGANIZATIONS

Assistance Dogs International
P.O. Box 5174
Santa Rosa, CA 95402
(610) 869-4902
Web site: http://www.assistancedogsinternational.org

Association of Pet Dog Trainers
104 South Calhoun Street
Greenville, SC 29601
800-PET-DOGS (738-3647)
Web site: http://www.apdt.com

Canine Companions for Independence
124 Rancho Del Oro Drive
Oceanside, CA 92057
(760) 901-4300
Web site: http://www.cci.org

International Association of Assistance Dog Partners
38691 Filly Drive

Sterling Heights, MI 48310
(888) 544-2237
Web site: http://www.iaadp.org
National Association of Dog Obedience Instructors
P.O. Box 1439
Socorro, NM 87801
(505) 850-5957
Web site: http://nadoi.org

NEADS/Dogs for Deaf and Disabled Americans
P.O. Box 213
West Boylston, MA 01583
(978) 422-9064
Web site: http://www.neads.org

Pet Partners
875 124th Avenue NE, #101
Bellevue, WA 98005
(425) 679-5500
Web site: http://www.petpartners.org

VIDEOS

Clicker Magic! DVD
Karen Pryor Clicker Training
49 River Street, Suite #3

Waltham, MA 02453-8345
Web site: http://store.clickertraining.com/clmadvd.html
Top-rated video with instructions on clicker-training dogs.

Take a Bow Wow and Bow Wow Take 2 DVD
Take a Bow Wow/North Star Canines
Web site: http://www.takeabowwow.com/products
Instructions for clicker-training dogs to do 21 "tricks,"
    from rolling over to turning the lights on and off.

WEB SITES

Due to the changing nature of Internet links, Rosen Publishing has developed an online list of Web sites related to the subject of this book. This site is updated regularly. Please use this link to access the list:

http://www.rosenlinks.com/CCWC/Anim

CHAPTER 5

WORKING AS AN ANIMAL HANDLER

While some police officers rescue abused animals, others work with animal partners. Animals also play vital roles in the military, in search and rescue operations, and as crime scene investigators. These animals are often—but not always—dogs. Animals who work in these jobs are not pets. They are professionals. They take their jobs seriously. They often work as equals with their human partners. Do you have what it takes to enter into a working partnership with an animal—to become an animal handler?

POLICE DOGS: THE K-9 UNIT

A dog's sense of smell is at least twenty times better than a human's. This, plus their excellent hearing, makes dogs valuable in police work. They can locate bombs and sniff packages to detect drugs. They can detect people (both alive and dead) in burning or collapsed buildings and disaster areas. Arson dogs can detect the smell of tiny amounts of accelerants such as gasoline, showing that a fire was caused by arson.

Rex, a member of the U.S. Customs and Border Protection K-9 unit, sniffs for drugs in luggage at Dulles International Airport. There is a growing demand for trained drug-sniffing and bomb-sniffing dogs.

Dogs can track and locate criminals and missing persons. Sometimes, they help crime scene investigators by detecting evidence that ties a criminal to a crime scene. In one case, a serial killer was caught because he owned cats. A dog from the K-9 unit traced the scent of the cats' hair to the bodies of the killer's victims, leading to his arrest.

Most K-9 dogs are German shepherds. Many are rescued from shelters. The dog's partner should be a police officer for at least a year before transferring to a K-9 unit. Many volunteer with the K-9 unit and then apply for positions as they open up. The dog and police officer must go through a six-month training course together.

POLICE HORSES

Some police officers partner with horses. Mounted police officers are highly effective because they are so easily approachable. Jim Barrett is a retired police officer who now trains police horses and their riders. He says, "Nobody wants to pet a police car."

Training police horses mostly involves desensitizing them to traffic noises, obstacles, vehicles, and people—whatever they will encounter in their daily routines. Horses are easily startled and hate loud noises. So, desensitization is both difficult and absolutely necessary. The main requirement for a human partner, besides prior police

On September 17, 2012, mounted police cross Wall Street in New York City. They are patrolling a protest marking the one-year anniversary of the Occupy Wall Street movement.

experience, is—not surprisingly—familiarity with horses and the ability to ride.

DOGS IN THE MILITARY

Although soldiers no longer ride horses into battle, animals still play a vital role in military operations. Horses are now mostly used for show, in parades and at military funerals. But other animals are on the front lines. The military has its own

On October 2, 2011, Corporal Mackenzie Richards, a military working dog handler with the U.S. Marine Corps, walks with John, an explosives detection dog, in Helmand Province, Afghanistan.

K-9 units, and its dogs have some of the same duties as they do in police forces. But they also have other more dangerous jobs. Recently, working dogs have served in the wars in Iraq and Afghanistan. Zzarr, a Dutch shepherd, is trained to detect bombs and improvised explosive devices (IEDs). Britt, a German shepherd, detects bombs and IEDs and is trained as an attack dog. Dasty, a Belgian Malinois, is trained to patrol and to locate a target individual. All three dogs have military ranks of sergeant or staff sergeant.

EXOTIC ANIMAL TRAINING CAREERS

Perhaps you love the idea of training animals, but you don't really want to work in law enforcement or the military. You could join the circus! Circus animals need care, grooming, exercise, and training. Or consider the animals in commercials, movies, and television shows, such as the animal documentaries on Animal Planet and NatGeo Wild. Someone has to handle and train those animals. Even if they don't do "tricks," the animals must be able to work with actors and be calm around lights and cameras. They also have to be fed, groomed, and cared for. Jobs like this would probably require you to relocate, but the more you learn about wild animals and the film industry, the more likely you are to find work in this field. This is one of the most exciting—and exotic—animal careers you could have.

A military working dog (MWD) handler is a member of the military who is first trained as a military policeman. MWD handlers in all services then go through the Air Force Dog Handler Team program. This program is run by the 341st Squadron at Lackland Air Force Base in San Antonio, Texas. Dogs and their handlers complete an intensive training program in either drug interdiction (detecting and revealing hidden drugs) or bomb sniffing. An MWD handler first enters the military, then passes basic training, is assigned to a military police unit, and finally completes the dog handler training program.

JOB PROSPECTS

Job prospects for dog handlers, both civilian and military, are excellent. In addition to working in police departments and military combat, trained dog handlers are needed to work for the Transportation Security Administration (TSA), a part of the Air Marshal Service. Dogs at airports do security checks of airline cargo, facilities, and luggage. They are vital in bomb detection. Dogs are also needed along the Mexican border, where drug smuggling is a major problem.

Animal handling is difficult and not for the timid. You must have not only a love for animals but also the skills and temperament to serve in law enforcement or the military. The training and work are intense, and the work environment is often frightening and dangerous. But together you and your animal partner can perform a vital service for your country.

WHAT IT'S LIKE

Military dogs go into dangerous areas before their handlers do, so they are even more likely to be killed or wounded. Since 2005, most members of the K-9 unit in Afghanistan have worn bulletproof vests. Navy Petty Officer 1st Class Michael Thomas served as assistant kennel manager for the 25th Military Police Company at Bagram Air Force Base. Thomas says, "These dogs are our partners. We travel with them, sleep with them and live with them. They are our best friends. Every dog handler will agree that there is nothing we won't do to protect our dogs."

FOR MORE INFORMATION

BOOKS

Bowling, Tracy. *Police K9 Tracking: A Guide for Training & Deploying the Police Tracking Dog.* K9 Publishing, 2010.
A complete manual on how to train and deploy police K-9s, including photos and diagrams.

Ritland, Michael, and Gary Brozek. *Trident K9 Warriors: My Tale from the Training Ground to the Battlefield with Elite Navy SEAL Canines.* New York, NY: St. Martin's Press, 2013.
A Navy SEAL's story of training dogs for the battlefield, with an inside look at the dogs themselves.

Schettler, Jeff. *K-9 Trailing: The Straightest Path.* Loveland, CO: Alpine Publications, Inc., 2012.
The difficulties of training "trailing dogs"—those who find people.

Smart Kids Series. *The K-9 Team: Top Dogs of the CIA.* First ed. Smart Kids Publishing, sold by Amazon Digital Services, Inc., Kindle edition, 2012.
This book provides a sneak peek at dogs the CIA uses to sniff out explosives; they can recognize 19,000 distinct smells.

ORGANIZATIONS

National Animal Control Association (NACA)
101 N. Church Street
Olathe, KS 66061
(913) 768-1319
Web site: http://www.nacanet.org
The NACA offers dog-training courses for animal control
   officers.

National K-9 Dog Trainers Association
221 Morrison Road
Columbus, OH 43213
(614) 864-8808
Web site: http://www.nk9dta.com
This organization offers dog training for family, service,
   industry, therapy, sport, and entertainment.

WEB SITES

Due to the changing nature of Internet links, Rosen
Publishing has developed an online list of Web sites
related to the subject of this book. This site is updated
regularly. Please use this link to access the list:

http://www.rosenlinks.com/CCWC/Anim

CHAPTER 6

WORKING IN ANIMAL AGRICULTURE

The importance of farming can't be overrated—after all, it's where all of our food comes from. Today, only two of every one hundred people work in farming, so you might think there are few jobs available. But if you know where to look, there are jobs. Many of today's farms are huge agribusiness operations specializing in one or two products, such as dairy, beef, or poultry farms. The small family farm is also making a comeback. Small farms don't make much money, and often, one member of the household has an outside job.

Animal farmers usually specialize in one type of animal. Dairy farmers raise cows for milk. Livestock farmers raise beef cattle, which are kept either in pastures or feedlots. Poultry farmers raise chickens to produce either eggs or meat. Other farmers raise sheep for wool or meat. Still others work as beekeepers. They collect and sell honey and rent bees to other farmers who use them to pollinate crops. A rapidly growing type of animal agriculture is aquaculture—farming fish or shellfish.

WHERE CAN I WORK?

Where you work in an animal career depends on you. There are jobs everywhere there are animals—cities, small towns, rural areas, coasts, and national parks and forests. And there are jobs around the world, so you can combine your thirst for travel with your love of animals.

To work with pets or domesticated animals, try animal shelters or humane societies, including rescue organizations. Or look for jobs with animal trainers, on farms or ranches, in veterinary clinics or hospitals, in kennels, or in retail pet shops. If wild or exotic animals are your thing, look for work in zoos or aquariums, wildlife centers (including rescue and rehabilitation centers), national parks or forests, or adventure parks such as SeaWorld or Six Flags.

And of course, you can always start your own animal business.

FARM OR STABLE HAND

If you live in a rural area, or can move to one, you can become a farm worker or stable hand on a large farm or ranch. Farm or stable hands make sure animals are fed and watered, move them from place to place as needed, and observe them for health problems or injuries. They also clean out barns or stables, repair fences and machinery, and perform other jobs to keep the farm or ranch running smoothly.

Farmer Tanner Rowe raises beef cattle on his farm outside Dallas Center, Iowa. Although farming is labor-intensive and often financially insecure, it is an essential and rewarding profession.

Farm and stable hands usually live on the farm or ranch. They eat meals there and receive a small salary. To do this job, you must be strong and willing to work hard, love the outdoors, and be ready for long hours and dirty work. Of course, you should be comfortable around large animals. It's also useful to know how to ride a horse and how to fix farm equipment. If this job appeals to you, you can begin right out of high school (or before, as a weekend or summer hand). You can learn on the job and work your way up to more responsible duties.

POULTRY JOBS

Most poultry, especially chickens and turkeys, are raised by intensive farming. That is, they are crowded together very closely with little room to move. Jobs can include receiving and sorting baby chicks, feeding chickens, cleaning pens or cage areas, and inspecting chickens for disease. If they are raised for eggs, the eggs must be collected. Poultry jobs pose some health risks. Workers should wear masks. If you have asthma or allergies, this is not the job for you.

EDUCATION REQUIRED

Those who grow up on farms begin their training as children by doing chores. Often, they join the local 4-H club, where they raise their own steer, pig, or chickens for sale. In high school, they might join the National Future Farmers of America organization (FFA). But you don't have to grow up on a farm. You can still join 4-H and FFA. You can visit local farmers and get hired for the summer or for evenings and weekends. Work hard, ask questions, and learn from experience and you can get a full-time job after high school. If you want to own your own farm, you should take agriculture and business courses in high school and vocational school. Computer knowledge and bookkeeping are important for keeping farm records.

JOB PROSPECTS

According to the U.S. Bureau of Labor Statistics, the demand for farm workers is decreasing slightly. Large farms are becoming

Organic farming is a growing industry and a potential source for employment. Here, a farmhand feeds geese at Moon in the Pond Farm, Sheffield, Massachusetts.

more efficient and need fewer workers. Also, farming is difficult, and many farmers lose money every year. Some go out of business. But there is still a need for farm workers.

Job prospects for aquaculture will be greater than for "conventional" animal farming. Most of today's seafood is imported or raised wild, so there is room for growth in fish farming. Also, organic, sustainable farming methods are gaining ground. People are more concerned about food quality and the environment. This means a greater demand for organically produced milk and free-range cattle and chickens. So if you don't mind hard work and living on the land is important to you, give farming a try. Just don't expect it to be easy!

WHAT IT'S LIKE

A high school sophomore in a small Nebraska town, Doug earns money doing everything from helping his neighbors move cattle to selling llamas. His main job, however, is at a local dairy. The dairy has six hundred head of cattle, which need milking twice a day. "Sometimes there's no rhyme or reason for when they need me," says Doug. "They just call and I go to work." His eight- to ten-hour shifts usually occur early in the morning or late at night. He milks, feeds, calves—just about everything a full-time professional dairy farmer does. He works so hard he's developed a reputation. "People say I have a good work ethic," says Doug. "And that makes me feel great."

It's "standing room only" for these turkeys on a Sonoma, California, farm. This intensive form of agriculture is typical for poultry farms, but many people consider it animal abuse.

FOR MORE INFORMATION

BOOKS

Bernstein, Sylvia. *Aquaponic Gardening: A Step-by-Step Guide to Raising Vegetables and Fish Together*. Gabriola Island, BC, Canada: New Society Publishers, 2011.
An ecologically sound method of farming fish and vegetables together.

Damerow, Gail. *The Backyard Homestead Guide to Raising Farm Animals*. North Adams, MA: Storey Publishing LLC, 2011.
Meant for people growing their own food, rather than making a living, but great information on how to choose and care for the right breed of animals.

Flottum, Kim. *The Backyard Beekeeper–Revised and Updated: An Absolute Beginner's Guide to Keeping Bees in Your Yard and Garden*. Minneapolis, MN: Quarry Books, 2010.
General information on bees and beekeeping, with beautiful illustrations.

MAGAZINES

Aquaculture North America
4623 William Head Road
Victoria, BC V9C 3Y7

Canada
(250) 474-3982
Web site: http://www.aquaculturenorthamerica.com
Trade newspaper for aquaculture in North America;
 information on technology, farm profiles, fish species,
 health, feeding, and more.

Bee Culture, The Magazine of American Beekeeping
P.O. Box 706
Medina, OH 44258
(800) 289-7668
Web site: http://www.beeculture.com
Designed for beginning beekeepers who want the latest
 information.

Farming Magazine
P.O. Box 85
Mt. Hope, OH 44660
(800) 915-0042
Web site: http://www.farmingmagazine.net/index.htm
Ecologically conscious farming on a small scale.

Progressive Dairyman
(800) 320-1424
Web site: http://www.progressivedairy.com
Has information on all aspects of dairy production.

Sheep! Magazine
145 Industrial Drive
Medford, WI 54451
(800) 551-5691
Web site: http://www.sheepmagazine.com
Topics on sheep and sheep farming for people at all
    levels of experience.

Small Farm Today
Missouri Farm Publishing, Inc.
Ridge Top Ranch
3903 West Ridge Trail Road
Clark, MO 65243
(800) 633-2535
Web site: http://www.smallfarmtoday.com
How-to magazine for traditional and alternative crops
    and livestock and rural living.

ORGANIZATIONS
Alternative Farming System Information Center
National Agricultural Library USDA
10301 Baltimore Avenue, Room 132
Beltsville, MD 20705
(301) 504-6559
Web site: http://afsic.nal.usda.gov

American Farm Bureau Federation
600 Maryland Avenue SW, Suite 1000W
Washington, DC 20024
(202) 406-3600
Web site: http://www.fb.org

American Society of Farm Managers and
Rural Appraisers
950 South Cherry Street, Suite 508
Denver, CO 80246-2664
(303) 758-3513
Web site: http://www.asfmra.org

Center for Rural Affairs
145 Main Street, P.O. Box 136
Lyons, NE 68038
(402) 687-2100
Web site: http://www.cfra.org

4-H Youth Development Organization
United States Department of Agriculture
1400 Independence Avenue SW, Stop 2201
Washington, DC 20250-2225
(202) 720-4423
Web site: http://www.4-h.org

National Future Farmers of America
P.O. Box 68960
6060 FFA Drive
Indianapolis, IN 46268-0960
(317) 802-6060
Web site: https://www.ffa.org/Pages/default.aspx

WEB SITES

Due to the changing nature of Internet links, Rosen Publishing has developed an online list of Web sites related to the subject of this book. This site is updated regularly. Please use this link to access the list:

http://www.rosenlinks.com/CCWC/Anim

CHAPTER 7

WORKING WITH HORSES

There are many ways to turn your love of horses into a rewarding career. You've already read about several. But if you really want to be a part of the "horse world," you might consider careers where you can work full-time at a stable or racetrack. This might be a small private stable where you groom horses or teach others to ride. Or it might be a large horse-racing business with many employees. Here, you might start out cleaning stables or brushing down horses. But, with increasing skill and experience, you can move up.

GROOM

Learning to groom horses is a great way to start your career in the industry. Grooms can find work wherever there are horses, including stables, farms, racetracks, riding schools, stud farms, boarding facilities, and even with large-animal veterinarians.

As a groom, your daily duties will usually include feeding and watering the horses and making sure they receive required supplements and medications. You'll wash and brush the horses, combing and detangling their manes and tails. You'll check them for signs of disease or injury and report problems to the trainer or stable manager. You'll care for the horses' hooves. You must also clean out stalls, add new bedding, and clean and maintain the tack (harnesses, bridles, and saddles). You are responsible for saddling and unsaddling the horses. As you gain more experience, you may also help with training, breeding, and foaling.

Groom Nanette Josey exercises a racehorse, One Only Knows, and her foal on a farm in Lexington, Kentucky. Kentucky is a center for horse breeding and racing.

Grooms usually need a high school diploma and a good knowledge of horses to get started. Much of your training will be on the job, through apprenticeships with experienced grooms or trainers. Some agricultural and technical colleges also offer training and apprenticeships. If you work at a race-track, you may become a trainer or even a jockey.

WRANGLER

At a ranch or stable, wranglers perform many of the same tasks as grooms. They also train horses. They ride the horses daily, teaching them to be comfortable with a saddle. They teach them to walk, trot, canter, gallop, and stop on command.

There's still a place for cattle wranglers, even in our highly urban society. Here, a wrangler prepares to lasso a cow and separate her from the herd.

On a ranch, wranglers usually herd and round up cattle or sheep. They work with a partner and sometimes a trained herding dog.

Some wranglers lead organized pack trips into wilderness areas. They usually work for companies that specialize in outdoor adventures. They load food and camping gear onto the horses. They introduce their clients to the horses and teach them how to steer and stop. Sometimes they also set up camp and cook. Other wranglers lead shorter, one-day trips called trail rides. They must be able to handle several horses at once and help people who have never ridden a horse.

EQUINE MASSAGE THERAPIST

If you're strong and physically fit and love working closely with horses, you can become an equine massage therapist. Just like a human massage therapist, you will massage the horses' muscles to work out kinks. Massage therapy loosens the muscles and improves circulation, stamina, and range of motion. It can help rehabilitate injured horses by loosening scar tissue and aiding healing. Massage also relaxes the horse. The only tool you will need (besides your own muscles) is a stool to reach the high places on the horse.

Some equine massage therapists are first trained in human massage. But you must become certified in either equine or animal massage therapy. You must take a course or program

A good massage relaxes a horse, just as it does a human. Here, Mercedes Clemens, an equine massage therapist in Maryland, massages her horse, Chanty.

approved by the National Certification Board for Therapeutic Massage and Bodywork. You can be certified for equine therapeutic or sports massage therapy. One typical program is five days long and includes both classroom and practical study. Most equine massage therapists take courses throughout their careers. Many are self-employed. But before starting your own business, it's best to gain practice and experience through an apprenticeship or by working for a business that does equine massage.

JOB PROSPECTS

Job prospects for working with horses range from fair to good, depending on the type of job and the area of the country. Obviously, regions with stables, stud farms, and racetracks will have the most opportunities. Grooms, wranglers, and, increasingly, equine massage therapists are needed wherever there are horses. Wages increase with experience. All of these fields require skill, determination, and stamina as well as a love of horses.

WHAT IT'S LIKE

Jen, an equine massage therapist from Fort Collins, Colorado, says:

> I am twenty-seven years old and have twenty years of experience riding and training horses. Last year I completed a two-week certification program in equine sports massage therapy through a company in Loveland, Colorado. The program gave me the skills to practice equine sports massage therapy on my own.

Massage therapy has put me on a whole new level with horses. All horses appreciate having their muscles rubbed. When you start massaging a horse, they sometimes start fidgeting, but when they realize that it feels really good, they settle down and show clear signs of comfort and pleasure. They push into you for more pressure, let their heads drop, and move around less. When I see this, I know I'm helping.

Owners tell me their horses perform better and feel better to ride after a massage. Horses are work animals—they jump, race, chase cattle, do dressage, or make tight turns around barrels. Caring for their muscles is key to keeping them fit and healthy.

FOR MORE INFORMATION

BOOKS

Freem, Kiki. *Clicker Training for Fun with Horses: Fun and Functional Horse Tricks for a Better Bond with Your Horse.* CreateSpace Independent Publishing Platform, 2012. Describes how to clicker-train horses in easy-to-understand language.

Masterson, Jim, and Stephanie Reinhold. *Beyond Horse Massage: A Breakthrough Interactive Method for Alleviating Soreness, Strain, and Tension.* Chicago, IL: Independent Publishers Group (Trafalgar Square Books), 2011. Step-by-step instructions for horse owners to use massage in improving performance.

O'Meara, Brendan. *Six Weeks in Saratoga: How Three-Year-Old Filly Rachel Alexandra Beat the Boys and Became Horse of the Year.* Albany, NY: State University of New York Press, 2011. Gives a behind-the-scenes look at the horseracing world and one particular filly.

Pelicano, Rick, and Lauren Tjaden. *Bombproof Your Horse: Teach Your Horse to Be Confident, Obedient,*

and Safe, No Matter What You Encounter. Chicago, IL: Independent Publishers Group (Trafalgar Square Books), 2004.
A manual, with illustrations, of how to teach horses to handle the unexpected.

Tucker, Renee. *Where Does My Horse Hurt? A Hands-On Guide to Evaluating Pain and Dysfunction Using Chiropractic Methods.* Chicago, IL: Independent Publishers Group (Trafalgar Square Books), 2011.
Uses color photos and diagrams to show owners how to detect their horse's pain and discomfort.

MAGAZINES

The American Quarter Horse Journal
American Quarter Horse Association
1600 Quarter Horse Drive
Amarillo, TX 79104
(806) 376-4811
Web site: http://aqha.com/journal
Up-to-date information and articles on American quarter horses.

Equus
Equine Network

656 Quince Orchard Road, Suite 600
Gaithersburg, MD 20878
(301) 977-3900
Web site: http://www.equisearch.com/magazines/
    equus
Articles on horse health, horse care, and other topics
    related to horses.

The Horse: Your Guide to Equine Health Care
P.O. Box 919003
Lexington, KY 40591-9003
(800) 582-5604
Web site: http://www.thehorse.com
Articles on all aspects of horse health and care, plus
    news on famous horses.

Horse & Rider
Equine Network
656 Quince Orchard Road, Suite 600
Gaithersburg, MD 20878
(301) 977-3900
Web site: http://www.equisearch.com/magazines/
    horse-and-rider
Articles on riding, choosing a horse, horse personali-
    ties, boarding, and other horse topics.

Horse Illustrated
P.O. Box 12106
Lexington KY 40580-2106
(800) 538-3000
Web site: http://www.horsechannel.com/horse
  -magazines/horse-illustrated
Horse care, riding, and training for all breeds.

Practical Horseman
Equine Network
656 Quince Orchard Road, Suite 600
Gaithersburg, MD 20878
(301) 977-3900
Web site: http://www.equisearch.com/magazines/
  practical-horseman
Articles on training and riding horses in competition.

Western Horseman
Western Horseman, Inc.
2112 Montgomery Street
Fort Worth, TX 76107
(817) 737-6397
Web site: http://westernhorseman.com
Covers a wide variety of horse-related topics, including
  health care, training, breeding, ranching, and more.

MOVIES AND VIDEOS

Equisearch.com
http://www.equisearch.com/resources/video
Videos and webinars on health issues, grooming,
    training, and more.

HorseChannel.com
http://www.horsechannel.com/horse-videos
Videos on horse health care, riding, training, and
    breeds.

Horse Health Videos
http://www.thehorse.com/videos
Includes videos, seminars, webcasts, and interviews
    on horse health; requires sign-in.

ORGANIZATIONS

International Association of Animal Massage and
    Bodywork
3347 McGregor Lane
Toledo, OH 43623
(800) 903-9350
Web site: http://www.iaamb.org/home.php

International Association of Equine Sports Massage
   Therapists
Web site: http://www.iaamt.com

New York Thoroughbred Horsemen's Association, Inc.
P.O. Box 170070
Jamaica, NY 11417
(718) 848-5045
Web site: http://www.nytha.com/benevolence/
   education.aspx

WEB SITES

Due to the changing nature of Internet links, Rosen
Publishing has developed an online list of Web sites
related to the subject of this book. This site is updated
regularly. Please use this link to access the list:

http://www.rosenlinks.com/CCWC/Anim

CHAPTER 8

WORKING IN A ZOO OR AQUARIUM

There's a lot more to the animal world than cats, dogs, cows, and horses. More than a million species of exotic animals, large and small, live in the wild. But the "wild" is shrinking rapidly as people cut, plow, and pave natural areas. Where do wild animals go, and how do we learn about them? Examples of many wild species are kept in the world's zoos and aquariums.

Zoos and aquariums are refuges for many endangered species. They allow people who would otherwise never encounter these animals to see and learn about them up close. They provide educational programs and shows to display animal behaviors. Many zoos conduct breeding programs to preserve animals and increase wild populations. Does this type of work appeal to you? If so, you might consider a career working in a zoo or aquarium.

ZOOKEEPER

All of those exotic animals, from elephants to tigers to seals, must be fed and cared for. That is the job of zookeepers and

This red panda is part of the Species Survival Initiative at the Vilas Zoo in Madison, Wisconsin. Zoo officials hope the panda and its mate will produce offspring to help save the species.

their assistants. At a small zoo, you might care for many types of animals. At a larger zoo, you will probably specialize in one type of animal. A zookeeper's duties are varied and sometimes dangerous. Remember, these are wild animals.

Many of them are large and strong. Some are predators, and all are unpredictable.

You must first make sure the animals are fed and watered daily. Food must be cut up and weighed. The animals are fed on a strict schedule and they must have clean water. Cages or enclosures are cleaned daily, and fresh bedding is added. Sometimes you clean the animals themselves—for example, elephants are hosed down daily. You also monitor animals for signs of illness or injury. This means watching and listening for changes in mood and behavior. If you see changes, you must notify the head keeper at once.

With experience and on-the-job training, you can increase your responsibilities by helping train the animals or educate the public. Wild animals cooped up in small spaces are often bored. Zookeepers try to improve their lives by providing them with stimulation. This may be as simple as hiding food or giving them toys to play with. But sometimes they train them to do certain behaviors—for example, they train primates to open their mouths wide or elephants to lift their feet. These behaviors help veterinarians examine the animals. Animals such as seals, dolphins, and birds are trained to appear in shows. As you progress in your zoo career, you might begin answering questions or giving talks to school groups. You might talk about an animal's behavior and characteristics or about the need for conservation.

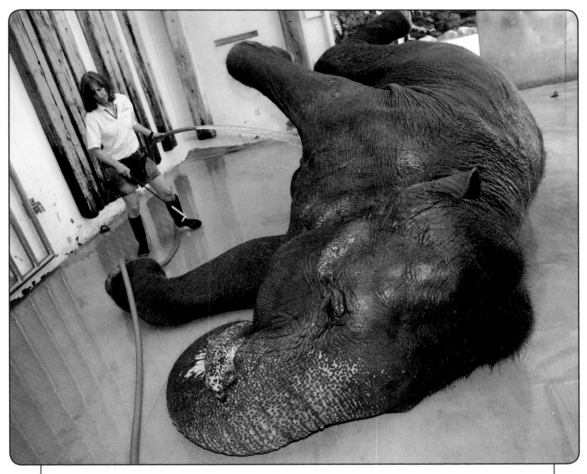

Everyone enjoys a good shower! A zookeeper washes down an elephant in Washington, D.C. Zoo workers must be comfortable working around large and potentially dangerous animals.

AQUARIST

Aquariums have similar functions to zoos—protection and conservation of animals and education of the public—but they concentrate on only aquatic animals. Your job as an aquarist will therefore consist of feeding and caring for animals in tanks or pools. These animals might range from tiny, brightly colored coral reef fish to huge sharks to friendly dolphins. As in a zoo, you must feed the animals and keep careful records of each feeding. For large tanks, you must don scuba gear, enter the tank, and feed the fish by hand! While in the tank, you check them for signs or illness or injury.

Part of the aquarist's job involves maintaining the tanks. This means preventing leaks. It also means monitoring water temperature and chemical content so the animals remain healthy. Tank filters must be checked, cleaned, and unclogged when necessary. Tanks must be scrubbed to remove algal growth.

Aquarists also do more exciting jobs. You might help design or build exhibits to make life more interesting for both animals and aquarium visitors. You might help train animals such as dolphins or sea otters to perform in shows. This often requires you to work in the water with the animals. In the process, you will learn a lot about animal behavior.

EDUCATION REQUIRED

Many zoos are simply looking for employees who love animals and don't mind working hard and getting dirty. You must be strong and in good physical condition. You must be able to handle yourself in a crisis. For example, what would you do if an animal escaped or attacked a visitor? Good math and communication skills are vital—you will be measuring animals' foods and interacting with the public. Any experience working with animals is a plus—from farm work to volunteering at a shelter. You should also be interested in conservation and preserving endangered species. Aquarists must also be strong swimmers and certified scuba divers.

JOB PROSPECTS

Job prospects are good for animal care workers in zoos and aquariums, but only fair for zookeepers and aquarists. You might have to relocate, but there are zoos and aquariums throughout the United States (and the world). If you get an entry-level job and do it well, you can work your way up. But in larger zoos or aquariums, you will have to continue your education to advance very far. This means college courses or a two- or four-year degree in animal biology or behavior.

WHAT IT'S LIKE

Bayley spent a summer as an intern at the Oregon Zoo in Portland. Here's how she describes her experience:

> Our day usually started with preparing food for the animals. I spent at least an hour cutting

Sea Biscuit, a green sea turtle, lost her left front flipper when injured at sea. She now lives (and swims with her three remaining flippers) in a tropical reef aquarium in Sydney, Australia.

up apples and sweet potatoes and spooning meat into bowls. After the animals were brought inside, I went to each exhibit, picking up animal droppings with a rake, shovel, or brush (depending on the animal). In the mountain goat exhibit, I had to scale the rocks with a rake and dustpan. We also had to pick up anything visitors dropped (or threw) into the exhibits.

Then, we fed and interacted with the animals. Before feeding, the keepers usually reinforced the animals' training. For example, the cougars and river otters had to show their teeth and paws before getting fed. This allowed the keepers to check for injuries.

YOU NEED PEOPLE SKILLS, TOO!

In most animal jobs, you'll also spend a lot of time dealing with people. If you work in a zoo, you'll be answering visitors' questions—and often preventing them from teasing or harming the animals. If you sell pet products, you'll be dealing with customers. If a pet is sick or is left at a boarding facility, the owners want to be sure the workers are caring and responsible. They want to know that their pet is in good hands. Other interactions, such as those involving pet rescue, may involve angry confrontations. You must be prepared to handle all situations with tact and courtesy.

One weird experience I had was making "cougar popsicles." The zoo's rhinoceros was a hemophiliac and was bled twice a week to keep him healthy. I was given a bag of semi-clotted blood and asked to fill balloons. I spent two hours covered in blood, filling balloon after balloon with rhino blood. I froze the blood-filled balloons and on a hot day, we peeled off the balloons and placed the "blood-sicles" in the cougar exhibit. The cougars loved their treat.

I loved interacting with the animals and finding new ways to enrich their lives.

FOR MORE INFORMATION

BOOKS

Brunner, Bernd. *The Ocean at Home: An Illustrated History of the Aquarium.* Expanded ed. London, UK: Reaktion Books, 2011.
Describes the history of the aquarium for the past one hundred-plus years, with illustrations.

Editors of *Time for Kids* Magazine. *Zoo 3-D: An Incredible Animal Adventure.* New York, NY: Time for Kids, 2012.
Beautiful 3-D photos of one hundred zoo animals, from big cats to exotic birds.

French, Thomas. *Zoo Story: Life in the Garden of Captives.* New York, NY: Hyperion Books, 2011.
Describes life behind the scenes at a zoo, including animal and human personalities and issues of captivity and conservation.

Laidlaw, Rob. *Wild Animals in Captivity.* Markham, ON, Canada: Fitzhenry and Whiteside, 2008.
Describes damage done to four animal groups (polar bears, orcas, elephants, and great apes) by confinement in zoos in unnatural spaces and inhospitable climates; for middle school age.

Nyhius, Allen W., and Jon Wassner. *America's Best Zoos: A Travel Guide for Fans and Families*. Branford, CT: The Intrepid Traveler, 2008.
Detailed descriptions of ten of the country's best zoos, arranged geographically.

MAGAZINES

Alive Magazine
NC Zoo Society
4403 Zoo Parkway
Asheboro, NC 27205
(336) 879-7250
Web site: http://www.nczoo.com/Membership/
   AliveMagazines.aspx
Quarterly magazine of the North Carolina Zoo.

Connect Magazine
Association of Zoos & Aquariums
8403 Colesville Road, Suite 710
Silver Spring, MD 20910-3314
(301) 562-0777
Web site: http://www.aza.org/azapublications
Articles on trends, education, and conservation efforts at zoos and aquariums.

Coral: The Reef and Marine Aquarium Magazine
Reef to Rainforest Media LLC
140 Webster Road
P.O. Box 490
Shelburne, VT 05482
Web site: http://www.coralmagazine.com
For marine aquarium hobbyists; has species profiles,
   information on setting up and keeping reef aquaria,
   technology, news, interviews, and beautiful photos.

Smithsonian Zoogoer
Smithsonian National Zoological Park
3001 Connecticut Avenue NW
Washington, DC 20008
(202) 633-2614
Web site: http://nationalzoo.si.edu/Publications/
   ZooGoer/about.cfm
Bimonthly magazine of the National Zoo, describing
   zoo activities, wildlife conservation, scientific research,
   and animal diversity.

ORGANIZATIONS
American Association of Zoo Keepers (AAZK)
3601 SW 29th Street, Suite 133

Topeka, KS 66614-2054
(785) 273-9149
Web site: http://aazk.org

Association of Zoos & Aquariums
8403 Colesville Road, Suite 710
Silver Spring, MD 20910-3314
(301) 562-0777

World Association of Zoos and Aquariums
IUCN Conservation Centre
Rue Mauverney 28
CH-1196 Gland
Switzerland
Web site: http://www.waza.org/en/site/home

WEB SITES

Due to the changing nature of Internet links, Rosen Publishing has developed an online list of Web sites related to the subject of this book. This site is updated regularly. Please use this link to access the list:

http://www.rosenlinks.com/CCWC/Anim

CHAPTER 9

WORKING IN WILDLIFE CONTROL, RELOCATION, AND REHABILITATION

When wildlife—a squirrel or raccoon, for example—decides to live in your attic or chimney, what do you do? You call a wildlife control and relocation specialist. This person can capture and relocate the misplaced animal to an appropriate place. When you find an injured hawk lying by the roadside, where do you turn? This situation requires a wildlife rehabilitator, who treats the animal's injuries and nurses it back to health.

WHAT WILDLIFE CONTROL PERSONNEL AND REHABILITATORS DO

Wildlife control and relocation specialists have two major jobs. First, they remove problematic wildlife from urban areas. Second, they try to prevent wildlife from reentering those areas by relocating animals to their natural environment. When they trap or handle an animal, they use humane techniques to avoid causing stress or injuries.

They may prevent animals from reentering homes by placing sturdy steel screens over potential entryways, such

as chimneys and vents. Or, they might deodorize a home to remove the animal's scent. This prevents other animals from coming to investigate. Once an animal is removed, it is relocated to a place such as a park. There it can be safe, find food and shelter, and live comfortably with other wildlife.

Wildlife rehabilitators care for wild animals that are sick, injured, or orphaned. Their goal is to return the animal to the wild when it is well again, not to tame it or turn it into a pet. They minimize human contact and do not try to eliminate the animal's fear of humans. Thus, the process involves some danger to the rehabilitator because the animals are frightened and often in pain. An animal that is too sick or injured to live successfully again in the wild may have to be euthanized. But if possible, it goes to an educational facility. There, it becomes an ambassador. It helps people understand and appreciate wild animals. Wildlife rehabilitators work with veterinarians, administer first aid, and do therapy to rehabilitate the injured animal. This often requires a long-term commitment.

You have to be fearless to do either job. The work can be dangerous—wild animals won't hesitate to bite or scratch if they're afraid or are trying to protect themselves or their young. You also have to be strong and healthy. You'll be working in all kinds of weather. You'll be carrying cages and moving equipment. You'll be on your hands

The game warden and animal control officers tranquilized this white-tailed deer before removing it from Angelo State University campus in San Angelo, Texas, and relocating it to a natural habitat.

and knees peeking into cracks and scrambling onto rooftops to inspect chimneys and vents. You'll also have to be good with people, as your customers will probably be right there with you. You'll need to be patient and be able to explain what you're doing.

EDUCATION REQUIRED

Many workers in wildlife control and relocation receive on-the-job training as apprentices. The National Wildlife Control Operators Association (NWCOA) offers a professional certification program for wildlife control workers. To enroll in the training courses, you must already be a professional. You must have experience managing wildlife damage and resolving conflicts between humans and wildlife. You need at least three years of experience to be fully certified. If you have less experience, you may be certified as an apprentice. The certification courses are challenging and you must continue to take courses throughout your career to remain certified. NWCOA also expects professionals to follow a strict code of ethics.

Certification is not required to work in wildlife control. You might learn everything you need to know through on-the-job experience. But certification gives you credibility, which will help in meeting your career goals.

As people encroach farther into animal habitats, more wild animals end up in cities and towns. Here, a California brown bear was tranquilized before removing it to a safer location.

JOB PROSPECTS

As the population grows, houses are built closer and closer to natural areas, which are homes of wild animals. Animals like raccoons and even coyotes and bears are increasingly appearing in populated areas. In the future, conflicts between humans and wildlife will continue to increase. More wildlife control and relocation specialists are needed to protect people and property and to protect wild animals from danger.

How easily you find employment and how much you are paid will depend on where you live, the specialized training you receive, and how big a problem animal/human conflicts are in your area.

WHAT IT'S LIKE

Lisette of Golden, Colorado, describes her work as a wildlife control and relocation specialist:

> I am twenty-six and work as a wildlife control specialist in Denver, Colorado. I have always loved animals. For two years, I volunteered at a local wildlife rehabilitation center to gain experience handling exotic animals. It was a wonderful feeling to help rehabilitate injured wildlife and release them back into the wild. I handled many different animals including raccoons, squirrels, foxes, beavers, and rabbits.
>
> I eventually realized I wanted a career in wildlife control and relocation. My current company responds to homeowners and businesses having problems with wildlife. Whether it's squirrels in the attic or skunks under the porch, we can help. I love my job and look forward to it every day. One of my first

jobs was to trap and relocate a raccoon living under a woman's back porch. Recently, I rescued an American kestrel (a small bird of prey) from a fireplace. I have also removed squirrels, bats, skunks, gophers, and beavers.

What I like most is that I'm helping both people and animals by safely relocating the animals to a new home and relieving homeowners of their worries. I love the fact that I never know what to expect from day to day. It's challenging to try to understand the behaviors of different species so I can figure out the best way to catch them. I would definitely recommend this type of work to anyone who loves animals, enjoys being outdoors, and likes the idea of having an adventure every day.

FOR MORE INFORMATION

BOOKS

Haynes, Diane. *Flight or Fight* (Jane Ray's Wildlife Rescue Series). Vancouver, BC, Canada: Whitecap Books Ltd., 2010.
Fiction series about a young teen who rescues a drowning seabird from an oil spill and becomes an activist; filled with details about wildlife rescue and rehabilitation.

Hentz, Peggy. *Rescuing Wildlife: A Guide to Helping Injured & Orphaned Animals*. Mechanicsburg, PA: Stackpole Books, 2009.
Instructions on what to do (and not do) when you find an injured animal.

MAGAZINES

NACA News
National Animal Control Association
101 N. Church Street
Olathe, KS 66061
(913) 768-1319
Web site: http://www.nacanet.org/nacanews.html

Bimonthly magazine giving information on issues
regarding animal/human relationships

National Wildlife
National Wildlife Federation
P.O. Box 1583
Merrifield, VA 22116-1583
(800) 822-9919
Web site: http://www.nwf.org/news-and-magazines/
national-wildlife.aspx
Magazine of NWF, dedicated to conservation and pro-
tection of wildlife and habitat around the world

Wildlife Control Technology Magazine
(860) 653-6933
Web site: http://www.wildlifedamagecontrol.net/
publications/wct.php
Bimonthly magazine for professionals in wildlife damage
control.

ORGANIZATIONS
National Animal Control Association
101 N. Church Street
Olathe, KS 66061

(913) 768-1319
Web site: http://www.nacanet.org/nacanews.html
National Wildlife Control Operators Association (NWCOA)
P.O. Box 3313
Fairfax, VA 22038-3313
(855) 466-9262
Web site: http://nwcoa.com

National Wildlife Rehabilitators Association (NWRA)
2625 Clearwater Road, Suite 110
St. Cloud, MN 56301
(320) 230–9920
Web site: http://www.nwrawildlife.org

USDA National Wildlife Research Center
4101 LaPorte Avenue
Fort Collins, CO 80521
(970) 266-6000
Web site: http://www.aphis.usda.gov/wildlife_damage/nwrc

WEB SITES

Due to the changing nature of Internet links, Rosen Publishing has developed an online list of Web sites related to the subject of this book. This site is updated regularly. Please use this link to access the list:

http://www.rosenlinks.com/CCWC/Anim

CHAPTER 10

BEING A PET GROOMER

Pet groomers are to cats and dogs what beauticians are to people. They are concerned with both the appearance and hygiene of the animals they care for. They untangle knotted fur. They cut hair to the right shape and length. They trim nails. They bathe and blow-dry. Do you love animals and have a knack for style? If so, pet grooming may be your calling.

WHAT PET GROOMERS DO

Groomers work in many different places, including kennels, veterinary clinics, animal shelters, and pet stores. Many groomers are self-employed. In addition to grooming, they must tend to business concerns like answering telephones, scheduling appointments, and paying bills. A relatively new trend is the mobile pet groomer. This person travels around, providing grooming services either in people's homes or out of a specially equipped van.

Grooming is particularly important for show dogs and cats. Each breed of show animal must be groomed to meet a specific standard. The groomer must know the specific cuts required for each breed and be able to groom the animal so it meets the highest show standards. The job can be stressful because those in charge of celebrity or show animals are very particular. Their animals are in the public eye and must look their best. Groomers in this field are paid very well.

During the grooming process, the pet is placed on a grooming table and brushed to remove loose dirt or twigs. Then the groomer trims the animal's nails and cleans its ears. She washes it thoroughly to clean the fur and remove fleas and ticks. The wash is followed by a thorough toweling or blow-dry. Then the groomer uses electric clippers and special grooming shears to cut the hair and a sturdy comb to untangle and pull the hair into shape. Some groomers then apply special powders and perfumes. When the groomer is finished, the pet is transformed.

EDUCATION REQUIRED

A groomer must love animals and be able to calm and soothe them. This means the groomer, too, must be calm and patient. The dogs and cats you see will often be shaggy, dirty, smelly, and shedding hair. You have to be able to see through the mess to imagine—and create—perfection.

No professional training is required, and most groomers learn on the job, as apprentices to an experienced groomer.

A Pomeranian sits patiently while a groomer trims his fur. Not all dogs will be this patient, so the groomer must be able to handle unexpected situations.

You can prepare yourself by spending time around pets—your own, your neighbors', or your friends'. Offer to groom your friends' pets for free. In high school, take courses in business, health, math, and science. If you plan to run your own grooming business, you'll need bookkeeping and office management skills. You need a great imagination to turn dirty creatures into works of art their owners will be proud of. Finally, read books on grooming and pet care.

YOUR FIRST RÉSUMÉ

Your résumé markets you to potential employers, so it should be perfect. Keep it short, and use bullet points. List all your relevant skills and activities, including education, clubs or organizations, offices you held, and special projects you did (such as organizing a fund-raiser). List all previous jobs, including volunteer work and internships. Even if you weren't paid, you did real work, gained important skills, and maintained a schedule.

Write a one-page cover letter to go with your résumé. Explain why you think you can do the job. Describe your most important credentials—for example, good grades in science classes or volunteer work at the local animal shelter. Describe how you feel about working with animals and how you can contribute. Always close by thanking them for considering your application.

Together, your résumé and cover letter should convince an employer that you are the best person for the job.

Approximately fifty pet grooming schools around the country offer training. The National Dog Groomers Association of America (NDGAA) offers workshops and certification. NDGAA workshops teach specific grooming techniques and proper styling techniques for different breeds. They also provide information on pet health care and on running your own pet grooming business. After graduating from either a grooming school or an NDGAA

A groomer brushes a fox terrier's coat. Brushing to clean and smooth the coat is part of the grooming process required to make a dog look his best.

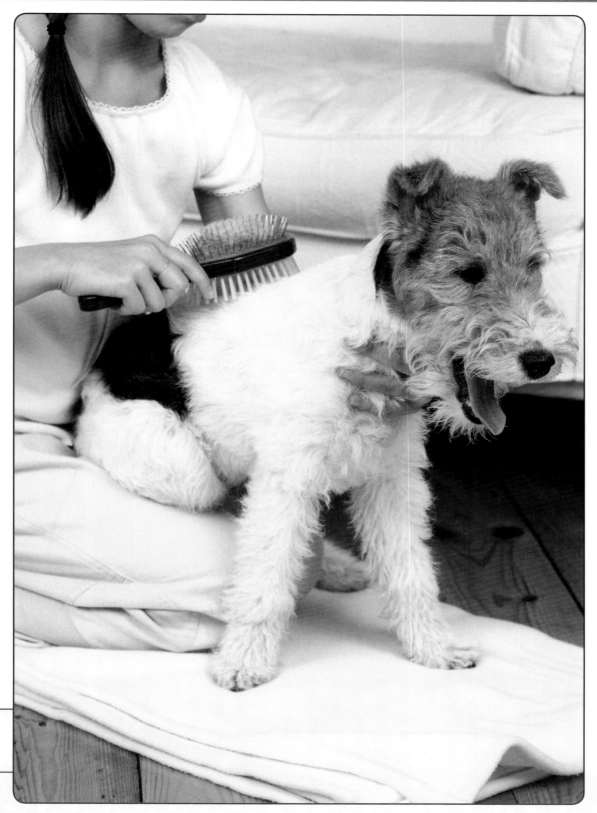

COOL CAREERS WITHOUT COLLEGE FOR PEOPLE WHO LOVE ANIMALS

workshop, you can take the NDGAA certification exam. Pass the exam and you'll be NDGAA-certified—a great addition to your grooming résumé.

You should also become a registered member of NDGAA. This shows you are serious about your grooming career. Most groomers continue to take workshops throughout their careers. And if you set up your own shop, you'll need an operator's license that meets local laws.

JOB PROSPECTS

In the future, there will be high demand for pet groomers. More and more people are buying and adopting pets—especially dogs—and more of them are willing to pamper their pets by paying for regular grooming. But the economy does influence the pet grooming business. In a good economy, when people have plenty of money, they tend to spend more on luxuries such as pet grooming. But when the economy is bad, the grooming business will slow down.

WHAT IT'S LIKE

Dawnita works as a pet groomer in a busy "all-purpose" animal care facility. Far in the back, behind the vet clinic, surgery, and kennel, is Dawnita's domain—a professional

116

grooming studio where she turns scruffy, shaggy animals into clean, neatly trimmed pets. Most of Dawnita's animal clients are dogs. She averages about eight full cuts per day, plus a few trims and washes. She also grooms four or five cats every week, most in the summer.

Most animals are easy to handle, Dawnita says. Only a few get annoyed. But after fourteen years on the job, she seldom requires help. In fact, she chooses to handle difficult animals by herself because she knows just how to calm them. She says there are two absolute requirements for a groomer—a lot of patience and a genuine love for animals. If you lack either one, she says, animals can tell. If the groomer is stressed, the animals will be too.

Dawnita especially likes caring for animals that were neglected or abused. She volunteers for a rescue group. "Cleaning and grooming dogs makes them feel so much better," she says. It also improves their chances of being adopted. A schnauzer that had been in the rescue center for weeks was adopted the day after Dawnita groomed him.

FOR MORE INFORMATION

BOOKS

Arden, Darlene. *The Complete Cat's Meow: Everything You Need to Know About Caring for Your Cat*. Hoboken, NJ: Howell Book House (John Wiley & Sons), 2011.
A complete guide to cat health and care, including a section on grooming.

Blackburn, Sandy. *The Everything Dog Grooming Book: All You Need to Help Your Pet Look and Feel Great!* Avon, MA: Adams Media, 2008.
A do-it-yourself guide to grooming your dog at home.

Dobish, Denise, Gay M. Ernst, Susan Gutman, Sandy King, Gloria Lewis, Risa Platau, Susan Tapp, Pat Wehrie, and Chelsea Youngblood-Killeen. *All-Breed Dog Grooming: Step-by-Step Illustrated Instructions*. Neptune, NJ: TFH Publications, 2011.
Dog grooming manual for professional dog groomers with excellent illustrations.

Gurman, Efroim, and Yanina Ruda. *A Comprehensive Manual for Individualized Dog and Cat Grooming*. Tree Media Inc., 2011.

Easy-to-read grooming handbook with detailed
illustrations and step-by-step instructions.

MAGAZINES

AKC Gazette: Digital Edition
American Kennel Club
8051 Arco Corporate Drive, Suite 100
Raleigh, NC 27617-3390
(919) 233-9767
Web site: http://www.akc.org/pubs/gazette/digital_
edition.cfm
Online monthly magazine with columns on each breed
and links to clubs for each breed.

Cat Fancy
Web site: http://www.catchannel.com/cat-fancy
Magazine of CatChannel.com; information on breeds,
judging, behaviors, health, rescue, and more; many
photos.

Dog Fancy
Web site: http://www.dogchannel.com/dog-magazines/
dogfancy/default.aspx

Magazine of DogChannel.com; information on breeds, judging, behaviors, health, rescue, and more; many photos.

eGroomer
Web site: http://www.northerntails.com/images/ egroomer_v1_issue_1.pdf
Online magazine giving information on the grooming business, including articles on (for example) pricing, shampoos, breed descriptions, diseases, and cat grooming basics.

Groomer to Groomer
Barkleigh Productions, Inc.
970 W. Trindle Road
Mechanicsburg, PA 17055
(717) 691-3388
Web site: http://www.groomertogroomer.com
Trade magazine for pet care professionals; includes grooming news, articles, and products.

The IPG Grooming Press Newsletter
6475 Wallace Road NW
Salem, OR 97304
(503) 551-2397

Web site: http://www.ipgicmg.com/IPG-Newsletters
--Directory.html
Newsletter of international organization that sets
standards for pet grooming; newsletter provides
updated information on certifications.

MOVIES AND VIDEOS

Doggie Cuts DVD
Dick Van Patten and Kevin M. DuVall
The Kevin Martin Corporation
Instructional video for grooming your dog at home.

Grooming Your Dog: Basic Haircuts DVD
MJM/A.R.T. Productions, Inc.
(818) 661-8483
Web site: http://mjmcompany.com/dvd-order.htm
Dog grooming instructions for both pet owners and
show people

Show Off Your Dog: Grooming Basics DVD
(818) 661-8483
Web site: http://mjmcompany.com/dvd-order.htm
Dog grooming instructions for both pet owners and
show people

ORGANIZATIONS

International Professional Groomers, Inc.
6475 Wallace Road NW
Salem, OR 97304
(503) 551-2397
Web site: http://www.ipgicmg.com

The International Society of Canine Cosmetologists
2702 Covington Drive
Garland, TX 75040
(972) 414-9715
Web site: http://www.petstylist.com/iscc/isccmain.htm

National Association of Professional Creative
  Groomers, LLC
P.O. Box 50
Childersburg, AL 35044-1880
(256) 378-6743
Web site: http://thenapcg.com

National Dog Groomers Association of America, Inc.
P.O. Box 101
Clark, PA 16113
(724) 962-2711

Web site: http://www.nationaldoggroomers.com/
   index.html

The Professional Cat Groomers Association of America
18839 Canyon Rd.
Fairview Park, OH 44126
Web site: http://www.professionalcatgroomers.com

WEB SITES

Due to the changing nature of Internet links, Rosen Publishing has developed an online list of Web sites related to the subject of this book. This site is updated regularly. Please use this link to access the list:

http://www.rosenlinks.com/CCWC/Anim

SELLING PETS OR PET SUPPLIES

Who doesn't love visiting a pet store? Whether it's a small local pet shop or a "big box" store such as PetSmart, they're always happy, welcoming places. There are puppies and kittens to pet and hamsters and guinea pigs to watch. There are chattering birds, exotic lizards, and colorful tropical fish. And of course, you'll find pet food, toys, pens and cages, furniture, kitty litter—in short, just about everything a pet owner could want or need. So if you really love the atmosphere of pet stores—the noise and excitement, smells, and interaction with both animals and people—this might be your career.

WHAT PET SHOP WORKERS DO

As a pet shop employee, you'll be part of a team of people selling pets and pet supplies to the public. On a typical day, you might stock shelves, take inventory, order new products, help customers, and clean up. You'll fill feed bins and set up sales racks and signs. You might have to sweep the floor and lock up the store at the end of the day.

If your pet shop sells animals as well as pet supplies, you'll probably have animal care duties. You'll clean out cages and aquaria, feed animals, and play with those that need exercise and human attention. In a small store, you will probably take care of all the animals. On a typical day, you might change the water in a fish tank, rearrange a turtle's habitat, or feed a hungry snake live mice for dinner. But in a large store, you'll probably specialize—working in the fish or bird department, for example.

You may also work in a position where you will have less direct contact with the animals, such as a stockroom supplier or buyer. This will help you learn about other aspects

A young boxer greets a pet store worker. Pet store workers must enjoy working with both human and animal customers, and they should be familiar with a wide range of pet products.

of the business. It will be valuable experience if you want to run your own pet shop someday.

EDUCATION REQUIRED

There is no special training required for pet shop workers. You can begin a part-time pet store job and receive on-the-job training while still in high school. To be employed full-time and to advance, you'll need a high school diploma. If you plan to run your own pet shop someday, you should study business, mathematics, and science in high school and, if possible, community college.

Besides a love of animals, you will also need good people skills. Most pet store jobs involve considerable interaction with the public. You should become very familiar with the products sold in the store so you can answer customers' questions. For any sales position, you need to be honest, dependable, courteous, and upbeat. You should have good sales skills and the ability to handle money.

If you can't get a job at a pet store right away, try to get animal and retail experience separately. Volunteer in another animal-based area (for example, at a shelter or a vet's office) and get a retail job in another field. Sooner or later, you'll be able to combine the two and find your dream job in a pet store.

JOB PROSPECTS

The pet and pet supply business is booming, and job prospects are excellent. Wages are usually hourly, beginning at minimum wage and increasing with experience. Chances for advancement are good. You might obtain experience and then move to a larger store, where your responsibilities and earnings will increase. You might also be promoted within the same store from sales associate to other positions such as floor manager, department manager, or eventually, even assistant manager or store manager.

WHAT IT'S LIKE

Trent got his job by being in the right place at the right time. He works at ClawPaws, a small pet shop with only three employees. How did he get the job? "I bought a snake here," Trent says. "Then I came in every week to buy it a mouse to eat. I was in here so often that when they had a job opening, they offered it to me!"

At ClawPaws Trent mostly cares for the reptiles. The others know more about the saltwater aquaria that cover an entire wall of the store. But everyone pitches in to do whatever is needed. "Learning about the fish has been hardest for me," Trent says. "You have to learn which fish are compatible." He

Pet store workers must have a good head for business, the ability to interact with people, and a willingness to care for and learn about many types of animals.

asks questions constantly and set up his own tank at home to learn more. Also, when the fish shipment arrives every Wednesday, he reads the names of each fish on the bag as he empties them into the tanks. That way, he learns to match the fish with their names.

Trent also loves taking care of the birds—particularly macaws. "They're very intelligent," he says. "You can tell they're trying to communicate. Being able to interact makes it very rewarding to care for them."

FOR MORE INFORMATION

MAGAZINES

Pet Age
Web site: http://www.petage.com
Digital magazine with helpful information for pet
  store owners.

Pet Business
333 Seventh Avenue, 11th Floor
New York, NY 10001
(646) 274-3525
Web site: http://www.petbusiness.com
Magazine designed to help pet retailers increase
  profits.

Pet Product News International
BowTie Inc.
P.O. Box 6050
Mission Viejo, CA 92690-6040
(949) 855-8822
Web site: http://www.petproductnews.com
Information on pet products, pet industry news,
  industry people, and profiles.

ORGANIZATIONS

American Pet Products Association, Inc.
255 Glenville Road
Greenwich, CT 06831
(203) 532-0000
Web site: http://www.americanpetproducts.org

Pet Industry Joint Advisory Council
1146 19th Street NW, Suite 350
Washington, DC 20036
(202) 452-1525
Web site: https://www.pijac.org

World Wide Pet Supply Association, Inc.
406 South First Avenue
Arcadia, CA 91006
(626) 447-2222

WEB SITES

Due to the changing nature of Internet links, Rosen
    Publishing has developed an online list of Web sites
    related to the subject of this book. This site is updated
    regularly. Please use this link to access the list:

http://www.rosenlinks.com/CCWC/Anim

CHAPTER 12

RUNNING YOUR OWN ANIMAL-BASED BUSINESS

You've just read about some exciting ways to build a career working with animals. Maybe some of them appeal to you, but you really want to be independent. You want to work with animals but still be your own boss. In other words, you'd like to start your own animal-based business. What kind of business can you start? Will it cost a lot of money? How will you find customers?

The type of business you start depends on you. What kinds of animals do you want to work with? Do you prefer pets, wild or exotic animals, large or small animals? Do you want to care for them, train them, teach about them, or photograph them? Do you want to sell pet items or work to save endangered species? In this section, we'll look at several examples of animal businesses that you can start with only a small investment.

PET SITTER/DOG WALKER

Pet sitting is much like babysitting—you are responsible for the pets' safety, health, and well-being while their owner is gone. You can begin pet sitting while you're still in high school. Ask neighbors and friends if you can watch their pets while they're away. You can even do it for free until you gain experience. A pet sitter must be extremely reliable and honest. You must know how to care for the animals, so you should get experience wherever you can—by caring for your own pets and by working or volunteering for any pet care business. You should also read books on animal care. Dog walking requires similar skills. But the owner may not be out of town. For example, you might walk dogs during the day while their owners are at work. And, of course, you can combine the two into a single career.

Dog walking and pet sitting are excellent businesses that you can start with a minimal investment. The demand is growing, and in big cities, dog walkers can earn up to $50 per hour.

But before you get into the job, realize that it is not easy. Pets get sick. They make messes on the floor. They fight with other animals. They lick you, shed on you, and get you dirty. And, even when there's a blizzard and several feet of snow on the ground, the dogs still have to be walked. If you have clients all over the neighborhood (or city), this can be a major hassle. Just be prepared, and realize it's all part of the job.

For either pet sitting or dog walking, you must follow the owner's directions carefully. Also, be sure you know whom to call in an emergency. Typical pet sitter duties include feeding, watering, walking or exercising, cleaning cages and kitty litter boxes, and giving medications. You'll be the pets' companion, and you'll be completely responsible for them until the owner returns.

In some cases, you might be asked to take care of the pet owner's house as well. They might ask you to pick up their newspaper or mail, turn the lights off or on, and water their plants. They might even pay you to spend the night to watch both the pets and the house. In this case, you can charge more.

If you make pet sitting or dog walking a full-time career, you should get certified through Pet Sitters International or the National Association of Professional Pet Sitters. PSI and NAPPS offer correspondence courses in animal health and care and how to run a business. While certification is voluntary, it gives you credibility and shows that you are serious and professional.

UNUSUAL PET BUSINESSES

Most people treat their pets as family members. This means a variety of new business opportunities for the animal lover. Demand for dog walkers and pet sitters is increasing. There are pet spas, doggie day-care centers, and bakeries that make and sell dog treats. There are designers of pet clothing and accessories. Pet relocation companies move your pets safely, even to other countries. People may become breeders of a particular breed or species. Experts at animal communication may become trainers. Opportunities for pet businesses are limited only by your imagination.

You should also obtain insurance in case the worst happens—for example, an animal gets lost or bites a neighbor.

ANIMAL PHOTOGRAPHER

Animal photographers specialize in photographing animals. Depending on their specialty, they can work in all types of environments. They might photograph lizards in the Southwest desert, bald eagles along the Alaska shores, breaching whales in the ocean, or lions in Africa. They might strap on scuba gear and use a special camera to photograph life on a coral reef. Or they might document happenings at circuses, zoos, or dog shows. There are photographers for just about any kind of animal.

The most common type of animal photography—and the easiest way to make a living—is to be a pet photographer. There are millions of pets in the country, and the demand for pet photography is growing. Some pet photographers have their own studios, with special backdrops on which they pose pets. Others visit the animals' homes and photograph them in their natural surroundings. Still others have mobile photography studios. Most photographers charge a sitting fee and then charge for copies of the photographs.

Good photographers work hard. They shoot hundreds of photos and spend hours digitally manipulating those photos to perfect them. A photographer must know how to operate a professional-quality camera. You must understand the entire

Adele Godfrey (*left*) heads a photo shoot for Animal Planet's "Puppy Bowl IX" in a New York City studio. Puppies and kittens on these shows come from shelters and rescue organizations.

photographic process, including how to set up and shoot artistic photos. Many skills can be learned in a photography class at your high school or community college. Practice is very important. Also, learn everything you can about the animals you're photographing. For dogs or cats, read up on different breeds.

Most animal photographers start by assisting an established photographer. Any experience will be valuable, even if it's not photographing animals. Working for an established company as a photographer gives you a steady paycheck and good experience before going out on your own. But photography jobs can be hard to land. It takes both persistence and talent to become an animal photographer.

WHAT IT'S LIKE

Yvonne owns Wings of Love, Inc., a performing bird company in Pleasant Hill, Missouri. Here Yvonne explains how she started her animal business and why she loves it:

> Much of my appreciation for birds probably came from visiting my grandparents on Sanibel Island in Florida. Escaped parrots, endangered cranes, herons, kites, tanagers, buntings, and shorebirds were everywhere. Then, my parents bought me a wild-caught Moluccan cockatoo, Snowball, in 1969. I still have him, and he's still very loving and healthy.

When I worked at a theme park, I took Snowball and two other parrots to work every day. People were fascinated by the birds' beauty and intelligence, and listened as I described the birds' plight in the wild from smuggling and tropical deforestation. Later I obtained more parrots, a toucan, and rare finches from around the world. We created a walk-through bird exhibit called Wings of Love. By this time, I wanted first-hand experience. I began visiting rain forests to learn more about the birds and their habitats. I took photographs of birds and wrote about my experiences.

Ten years later, when the theme park was sold, I constructed an elaborate sunroom for the birds and moved them home. I had been asked to bring the birds to schools, churches, and retirement homes, so I began training them for shows. Nobody has ever shown me how to train an animal. It's unbelievable, but they have learned to ride a high-wire bicycle, roller-skate, play basketball, bowl, speak on cue, and more. One of our parrots has a famous line: "I can talk...can you fly?"

We are the only performing bird show in the Midwest and we have been making a living at it for nineteen years. My life has been very blessed with the gift of utilizing these birds for education and environmental programs.

FOR MORE INFORMATION

BOOKS

Entrepreneur Press and Eileen F. Sandlin. *Start Your Own Pet Business and More* (StartUp Series). Irvine, CA: Entrepreneur Press, 2009.

Pflughoeft, Jamie. *Beautiful Beasties: A Creative Guide to Modern Pet Photography*. Hoboken, NJ: John Wiley & Sons, 2012.
Describes pricing, working with clients, and building a solid workflow.

Vaughan, Cathy. *How to Start a Home-Based Pet Sitting and Dog Walking Business* (Home-Based Business Series). Guilford, CT: Globe Pequot, 2011.
Simple step-by-step instructions on registering your business, getting insurance, marketing, expanding, and more.

MAGAZINES

Nature Photographers Online Magazine
Jim and Donna Erhardt, Publishers
Nature Photographers Network
P.O. Box 10601
Bedford, NH 03110

Web site: http://www.naturephotographers.net
Official site of Nature Photographers Network; focus on
   nature, wildlife, and landscape photography for all levels.

ORGANIZATIONS

National Association of Professional Pet Sitters
15000 Commerce Parkway, Suite C
Mt. Laurel, NJ 08054
(856) 439-0324
Web site: http://www.petsitters.org

Pet Sitters International
201 E. King Street
King, NC 27021
(336) 983-9222
Web site: http://www.petsit.com

WEB SITES

Due to the changing nature of Internet links, Rosen
Publishing has developed an online list of Web sites
related to the subject of this book. This site is updated
regularly. Please use this link to access the list:

http://www.rosenlinks.com/CCWC/Anim

GLOSSARY

APPRENTICESHIP A job-training period working with someone who is more experienced.

CAREER A profession or permanent job.

CERTIFICATION Formal recognition for having completed special training and met certain qualifications.

DIPLOMA A certificate that recognizes completion of and graduation from school.

EMPLOYEE One who works for an employer.

EQUINE Having to do with horses.

EUTHANASIA Humanely killing very sick or injured animals to end their suffering.

FREELANCE Working at a profession without a long-term commitment to any one employer.

HUMANE Friendly and compassionate consideration for animal welfare.

INDUSTRY A group of businesses in the same field.

NONPROFIT ORGANIZATION An organization that conducts business for the welfare of the general public without a profit motive.

PROFESSIONAL A person with a career.

RÉSUMÉ A summary of work experience, education, and skills.

SALARY A predetermined amount of money to be paid to an employee for a year's work.

SELF-EMPLOYED Working for oneself, not for an employer.

TECHNICIAN A specialist in the technical details of an occupation.

U.S. BUREAU OF LABOR STATISTICS (BLS) The government agency that keeps track of job trends in the United States.

VOLUNTEER One who willingly works without pay.

WILDLIFE REFUGE A place where wildlife can safely find shelter.

WILDLIFE REHABILITATION CENTER Place where sick or injured wildlife is cared for and brought back to health.

WORK ETHIC How hard a person works at his or her job.

INDEX

ABOUT THE AUTHOR

Carol Hand grew up on a farm and has always had pets, including cats, dogs, fish, and the occasional lizard. Currently, she owns four cats, all rescues. She has degrees in zoology and marine ecology, and now writes science books for children and teens.

PHOTO CREDITS

Cover, p. 3 zhangyang13576997233/Shutterstock.com; pp. 6-7 iStockphoto/Thinkstock.com; pp. 10, 12-13, 15, 89, 102, 105, © AP Images; p. 21 Julie Denesha/Getty Images; pp. 22-23, 54-55 John Moore/Getty Images; pp. 32-33 Helen H. Richardson/Denver Post/ Getty Images; pp. 35, 64-65 Bloomberg/Getty Images; pp. 42, 79, 135 The Washington Post/Getty Images; p. 46 Jeff Siner/MCT /Landov; p. 53 Paul J. Richards/AFP/Getty Images; p. 56 Cpl. Bryan Nygaard/U. S. Marine Corps photo; p. 67 Robert Nickelsberg/Getty Images; pp. 68-69 Justin Sullivan/Getty Images; p. 76 Lexington Herald-Leader/ McClatchy-Tribune/Getty Images; p. 77 Design Pics/Thinkstock; p. 91 Taylor S. Kennedy/National Geographic Image Collection/Getty Images; p. 94 Greg Wood/AFP/Getty Images; p. 113 David Joel/ Photographer's Choice/Getty Images; p. 115 Steve Lyne/Dorling Kindersley/Getty Images; p. 125 Boston Globe/Getty Images; p. 128 Fuse/Getty Images; p. 132 John Burke/Photolibrary/Getty Images; cover and interior design elements © iStockphoto.com/pialhovik (banner), © iStockphoto.com/David Shultz (dots), Melamory/ Shutterstock.com (hexagon pattern), Lost & Taken (boxed text background texture), Florian Augustin/Shutterstock.com (chapter opener pages icons).

Designer: Brian Garvey; Editor: Bethany Bryan; Photo Researcher: Amy Feinberg